# Towards Understanding

Lillian Brummet

PublishAmerica
Baltimore

First printing

ISBN: 1-4137-9337-1
PUBLISHED BY PUBLISHAMERICA, LLLP
www.publishamerica.com
Baltimore

Printed in the United States of America

# Towards Understanding

## Reviews:

"*Towards Understanding* by Lillian Brummet, is a book of soul-searching poetry spanning many experiences in the life of the author. We see life through her eyes as she has gone through many difficult experiences. Brummet has a true poet's eye for detail, description, and emotion and carries the reader along on her journey. Rather than deny or hide our past, we need to face and deal with the pain and sorrow in life in order to get beyond it to better things. It is obvious that while Brummet has indeed suffered, she has not only survived but thrived! I enjoyed reading this book and recommend it to others who enjoy soul-searching poetry!"

~ Michelle True, author of *True Reflections and True Emotions*

"I think this is some of the most gripping poetry I've ever read. Since it was presented somewhat in time sequence, I felt glued to the screen, wanting to know what happened next, as if reading a biography or diary or novel!

"It was clearly not written for the public, but for herself, and there is this total honesty about it. It tells about a young person, having fallen into total despair, feeling unloved, unwanted, but somehow making her way, crawling out of that dark hole of depression - advancing afraid, yet not willing to let the fear stop her."

~ Sonja Gartner - Reader

"Today I completed an emotional and sometimes haunting journey with a fellow author and friend, much to my good fortune. Lillian's collection of poetry touched many chords inside my soul and I am proud to have been given the opportunity to experience it before publication of this book. Many times you can read another's work and not begin to know them in any in-depth way at all. I truly feel that after reading this exceptional collection I have a new understanding of this author and in some ways myself.

"I felt truly inspired from sharing some of her darker moments such as in, "Bad Weather- But when I wake up to the dawn, I will remember all the pain - I will look around and scorn At each day spent in vain." Her messages of understanding and her zest for living comes through loud and clear in passages such as the one from, 'Joy of Living- So many dreams that could fail, I wonder if it is easiest to give up. No, the time for me to live is now.' The truth of all life is shared in this heartfelt sentiment within, 'Educated Lies' – 'This world is not forever, Life's just a one time deal.' Finally, her tribute to our Mother Earth is a celebration of all the environmental beliefs I hold dear as well in, 'How can they be so cruel?'

"I found so many passages within this collection that I felt an immediate and absolute connection with and many that I gained a new and brighter understanding from. I feel that this outstanding collection of very personal and sometimes painful work has all the makings of a great read. Kudos to the author for sharing not only her work but pieces of her heart and soul with her audience as well."

~ Tessa Crigger, author of *I Hear Gaea's Tears* (www.spiritofmotherearth.com)

"Mrs. Brummet takes you on a journey of her past life, a life that she worked hard at to stay afloat. I must say that during my reading of *Towards Understanding*, I realized that Lillian was able to touch on real feelings and real issues that are in our everyday lives. Her poetry makes you think, painting a picture of that moment she is describing. One of my favorites, 'Survivor,' reveals her inner strength with honesty.

"*Towards Understanding* is written with determination and reverence. Spilling her heart in words, Lillian shows that she is a fighter. A fighter, who endures several rounds and makes it a point to get back up, and face another challenge."

~ Marguerite Ashton, author of *Taylini - A Family Saga and Traci's Story* (www.ryze.com/go/bellarose26) (www.publishedauthors.net/margueriteashton)

"*Towards Understanding* is by far the most outstanding book of poetry that I have read, thus far. This amazing work of art starts with an introduction that gives a little insight into the life of Lillian, the author; then proceeds with the poetry that takes you into her heart. Like a blooming rose to completion you travel through her life as though it where your own, experiencing everything from fear, frustrations, and memories to love, purpose, and self-acceptance.

"I truly found something special that touched my heart in each and every piece of poetry in this book. This window into Lillian's' heart inspires hope, peace, and strength in a troublesome world like I would have not imagined. The words so beautifully written are those that can be read over and over again!"

~C.J. Wilkes, author of *Daddy, I Forgive You* (www.cjwilkes.com)

" 'There is but a child in me, waiting to escape. To see the wonders of the world, And rid herself of hate,' writes Lillian Brummet, in the poem 'Trapped', which illustrates a longing for the love she had not experienced during childhood. Lillian is a free-lance writer and her first full-length book of poetry entitled, *Towards Understanding*, adequately reflects this collection of poems in its entirety.

"I always find that when a poet's work is honest and filled with thoughts that each of us can empathize with or have experienced ourselves are the most appealing pieces to read. Every poem is a journal - a poetic diary that deals with trials and overcoming strife. Her muses genuinely articulate anger, love, disappointment, friendship and endeavors to understand others.

"Lillian's style of writings consists of mostly rhyme with a touch of free verse. My personal favorite is 'Bad Weather', not only because she cleverly uses nature as a metaphor to depict her mood, but also because she showed superb use of imagery when describing how gloom becomes tangled in her hair.

"This book is organized in chronological order according to the year in which the work was written. Those who like reading poetry that questions society and depicts true life experiences will enjoy this book of poetry."

~ Nadia Brown, author of *Unscrambled Eggs* and editor of *Liquid Muse*, an online poetry publication. (www.nadiabrown.com)

"*Towards Understanding* by Lillian Brummet is an absorbing and interesting collection of poetry, which displays the author's great depth of emotion. This book takes the reader on Lillian's journey of self-discovery. Her choice of words allows for the perfect visuals. I got a clear sense of her inner turmoil at the beginning of the book, as she so honestly expresses herself with skilled writing ability. As the poetry evolved chronologically, I was able to feel her personal growth. I enjoyed reading this book."

~ Debra A. Warren, author of *Pausing to Catch My Breath* (www.freewebs.com/deb_w/)

"*Towards Understanding* by Lillian Brummet, is a book that grabs your heart with poetry containing both love and hurt about life's experiences. I found Lillian's poetry a book I could pick up at anytime and feel comfortable visualizing her message. Her stories that seemed to pour out her life with nothing held back gave me inspiration and hope for all. As a writer being able to put feelings into words is the most difficult task we have, but Lillian does what most of us only dream about doing. The words made my heart shake, feeling things one seldom does. I am very impressed with Lillian's talent and can see her becoming a voice for readers world wide."

~ Ronald Nussbeck, author of: *The Deception*, *Retribution* and *The Coin*.

## Acknowledgments:

I would like to acknowledge my husband, Dave, for his enduring strength and protection, his kind and gentle soul, and his patience while I became absorbed in the creation of this manuscript. Dave is the proofreader for this book. He is my soul mate, my healer - my friend.

I feel it is also important to acknowledge Hildegard Boenisch, a poet in her own right, who helped me believe in and pursue my dreams. She is a gifted woman and brought to me the most pure friendship I have ever experienced. I love you both so very much.

Finally, I give thanks to my mother – for she has endured so much pain for her children. She is my long-distance friend and confidant – I love her dearly.

# Table of Contents:

# Introduction:

I would like to tell you a little about the history of my life – not because I want to hear a band of violins strike up a tune, but because I feel it is important for the reader to understand the author in order to relate to the poetry. I will be as brief as possible.

Like many others, my childhood turmoil spawned the beginning of my poetry writing. Home life was unstable for our family – we seemed to move from place to place all the time. When my mother immigrated the family to Canada to marry, I found it very hard to adjust. It did not help that this husband was one of the two who found me more interesting than they found my mother. I was sent to live at a boarding school for two years - for my own protection. I only saw my mother twice, I think, during that time. Both visits involved a long Greyhound bus ride all alone, which I did not relish. Both my brothers had left home by the age of 16, so I did not get to see them during those visits and I felt very lonely. Eventually, my mother found a way to leave her husband and a place for us to live together. However, we did not know each other well, and did not have the skills to deal with ourselves – let alone each other. One day I came home to find a bag of my things on the doorstep and a note. I was just over 13. For a while, I was able to sleep at various school friends' homes, but that did not last long. As soon as parents began asking questions, I knew I had to move on. I stayed all of two nights on a park bench before I received my first Orphan's Benefit check, (courtesy of my biological father), which was just over the cost of rent for a small apartment. Between that check and the various jobs I could get, I was able to stay out of the system, pay rent and even help some runaway kids for a time.

I was caught living on my own when I had to stay at the women's shelter for a few days at the age of 16. I was terrified they would send me into the foster home system, or worse. A social worker there looked kindly upon me and she took me into her home on the condition that I went to school part-time and at least finish 10th grade. I was still allowed some freedom and allowed to work. However, having been on my own already for so many years, I found it very awkward to be around a family doing family stuff. Therefore, I left as soon as I fulfilled our agreement. I have never forgotten Jan's kindness and counseling - for she helped me understand my rage and fear. Jan also brought my mother and I together, and though it took many years, we are close friends now.

As an adult my education continued and then, after some college courses I became involved in the hospitality industry. However, a vehicle accident ended that career. I then started a small business, which was successful for over seven years, but it too ended through a more serious vehicle accident. This time I had to choose either retraining for a part-time job that would accommodate my disabilities - or pursuing my dream of becoming a writer. I chose the latter.

## The Poetry:

This book has been organized in chronological order according to the year in which the work was written, beginning in 1987 when I was 17.

I began writing poetry about the age of 16, but that work does not appear in this book as it was too blue and angry for the public – in fact I completely deleted those files some time ago.

Poetry was one of the tools that I used to crawl out of hell. Never intending it to be read by others, it was my way of dealing with things. You will see me battle past demons, raise my voice in anger, discover self-awareness and recover from an intense relationship that bordered on obsession. You will witness the healing as I become aware of the value of my life. Finally, I begin to see beyond myself and start to question society and endeavor to understand others. I also discover a love for, and dedication to, the health of the Earth.

I hope that you will enjoy the journey as much as I have had fun experimenting with different writing styles and using different rhythms with words.

# WOMEN'S JEALOUSY

The girl in white lace and shiny gray stockings,
Attacks every man with her nightmarish taunting.
Her beauty is rare, her movements are sure.
Her casual flirting leaves minds in a blur.
Women both hate her and dote on her too.
They wish they could be that woman anew.
But they're only themselves - though jealous they be;
Thinking from women like that, no man would flee.
But she is covered in make-up, and shading, and light.
She will take many photos until she gets it just right.
These women wish with all of their foolish might,
That they forget who their man is with tonight.
As they wrack themselves over this orchestrated myth,
They enlarge the distance from the one they are with.

(1987)

# BREAK-UP

Being alone,
Is frightening – it is true.
It is knowing that there is no one;
There is only you.
The friends that were there,
Once sticking by you;
Just did not replace a thing.
Sex does not matter;
Does not cure being alone.
It only postpones familiar feelings,
Leaving hints of guilt and cheap cologne.
Yet making that move
Of commitment for two,
Is the most frightening feeling
That could come over you.

(1988)

# DREAMS

Sometimes I feel so lonely,
So damn tired of feeling pain.
Forever and ever, until death do us part;
Tell me what that really means.
Is it something that people say,
Just to fulfill their dream for the day,
Or is it a promise, they really feel,
And mean in every way?
It is a question no one can answer,
For no one really knows.
There are too many fools and jokers
Whose faces may be friendly,
Yet their hearts are cold.

(1988)

# CHERISHED MOMENTS

The friend you could count on.
The neighbor who was kind enough to care.
The stranger reaching out with his palm.
The giving beggar who was blind.
The warm car that gave a ride.
The one who was there just when you need.
The child's simple thoughtful deed.
The sun shining on a rainy day.
The peaceful harmony a song once brought.
The hidden lessons in every moment of every day...
Moments conveniently there when they are sought.

(1989)

# WORRIES

When worries come falling down,
From the cold unwanted clouds
And everything seems to sprout up,
From the cold and frozen ground.
When worries of tomorrow come;
With what strength? Where will I get it from?
And everything seems impossible;
Though I know it is commonly done.
When I'm feeling rough,
When things are getting tough,
Worries fall down like rain…
At times, I feel I have had just about enough.
I remember from where I have come…
Yet it brings no comfort to me.
And I think of how far I've gone;
And how much I have done… how much I have to do…
I remember all the joys, and pains;
And all the friendships lost and gained…
I think of possibilities…
But my fears keep me here…
…And I don't know what to do.

(1989)

# TRAPPED!

There is but a child in me,
Waiting to escape.
To see the wonders of the world,
And rid herself of hate.
She wants to feel joy in living,
And romantic summer eves.
She dreams of running wild,
Through autumn's fallen leaves.
But I keep her well inside;
Afraid of experiencing pain.
She shouldn't have to cry,
That sweet little child of mine.

(1989)

# THE FACE

You live your life in a frivolous way,
And it leaves you happy, in an unhealthy state.
Though you've tried all that you could;
It brought you only emptiness; loneliness.
You feel that you have lost yourself in a mindless fog
And that love will only leave you further in that bog.
So, you cover yourself with your bittersweet sass;
And you carry on your life remaining terribly sad...
Yet I can see through the face in which you are clad.

(1989) - Ode to Roxanne

# SOMEWHERE DOWN DEEP BELOW

Somewhere down deep below,
Feelings inside me multiply and sow.
The harder, colder feelings then enhance,
And outside, they are determined to show.
Sticking to all four sides, they take control.
Bouncing back and forth, the inner starts an echo.
Resounding lessons and sermons -
All mixed up words that reap confusion
As they bond and fill every hollow.

Somewhere down deep below,
The ability to love dimly glows.
It sends a shadow down the forbidden path…
And then one wall begins to erode.
One down, yet thousands to go…
Slower, yet steadier, the programmed feelings flow.
This endless battle has made the slightest advance,
Behold! The cycle has surely begun to slow!

(1989)

# BAD WEATHER

The sun is barely showing,
Between the matted clouds;
What a crabby, drabby day!
Gloom flows quickly downward,
And becomes tangled in my hair;
A brew of utter despair!
Cold wind seeps in my shelter,
And chills my aching heart.
Past and its insecurities,
Are tearing me apart.
The sun is now fading.
And the moon will soon arrive.
It will wrap me up in darkness,
And feed me only lies.
But when I wake up to the dawn,
I will remember all the pain.
I will look around and scorn
At each day spent in vain.

(1989)

# FOR TODAY, MY LOVE

Sometimes I wonder if you ponder,
Is it just tonight?
Or where we'll be tomorrow,
And what I have in sight.
Today, I do not feel lonely…
I am not crying in the nights.
But I'm not about to trust or love;
Over my unstable fright.
When you go I will not wait.
So, today, my love - don't feel too much.
I am sorry you are pushed away,
And I suffocate your touch.
But I am not ready for commitment.
And still not ready to forget…
So for today, my love - let's just enjoy,
And accept just what we get.

(1989) - Ode to Ken

# OF YESTERDAY, I DREAM

Of yesterday, I dream.
The happiness then, it seemed,
Would never really end.
Yet now, to live - I must pretend.
Helplessly, I slowly die.
In pain, I stumble, I fall…
My mind is slipping away…
My movements jerk and sway.
My children and husband have gone,
Leaving me to suffer alone.
Afraid, I hover in my dreams,
For I've only my walker, on which to lean.
There's so much I would change…
…Times I'd rearrange…
All my possessions I'd gladly give,
If one more yesterday, I could live.
I would a cure to come,
To save my defenseless corpse.
As this disease eats my muscles and bones,
I muffle my furious groans.
…In humiliation, I weep,
How fast this disease did creep!
And in night, I find my only haven…
My one comfort comes from sleep.

...I would to dream forever...
Where I have yesterday once more;
And never again would I have to take,
The disappointment, each morning I wake.

(1989) - Ode to Vicky, a good friend and victim of Multiple Sclerosis.

* Published in the local Multiple Sclerosis Society's Newsletter in 1989. Also published, 2003 in Kelowna's (sector of the society) newsletter June, 2003 newsletter.

# TERMS OF LIFETIME LOVE

I just want you to understand,
How I feel, for it is what I am.
I just want you to be around,
To be my one and only man.
I just want your trust and love,
For I just can't seem to get enough.
I just want you to lift me high,
And see through my bluff.
I just want you to understand,
To wrap us up in a silver band.
I just want you to be around;
And together, walk hand in hand.

(1989)
*Published 1999 in the Hardcover Anthology: *The Last Good-byes* - National Library of Poetry
*Editor's Choice Award for Outstanding Achievement in Poetry

# AFTERMATH OF LIFE

My eyes are open wider now,
My ears are not so closed.
My mind is much broader,
My speech is more composed.
I'll remember what I've been taught,
Until my dying day.
And I look forward to tomorrow,
While concentrating on today.
My goals are running higher in number,
My dream's about to grow.
But I can now look back and remember…
To use what I now know.
I acknowledge what must be done,
Though I still hesitate,
Because I fear that one step to renew me…
Will only dissipate.
Yet tomorrow, I begin to walk
Up the inclined path,
And struggle up the virtuous cliffs
'Til I reach life's aftermath.
The Aftermath of life I seek.
The payment for survival.
But 'til then, I have to walk.
On these poor and blistered feet.

(1990)

# EMPTY WORDS

Was it not just yesterday,
You smiled as my friend?
But how was I to know…
You found it so easy to pretend?
You left me solely standing,
In the hard falling rain.
Now I feel so deserted,
With this unrelenting pain.
Where did all those words go?
Did the wind just blow them away?
Or was it just a phrase
You rehearsed so well to say?
I believed in you, my friend,
And trusted you as well.
But under your facial layer
You're naught but an empty shell!

(1990)

# TEAR-SHINED EYES

Hi, it's me calling again, though only in my mind this time.
It is funny how I wonder how you are,
My god, am I totally blind?
I found a note in my drawer, and was left set back.
All my dreams began to blur - all my goals went slack.
And suddenly I was crying again, wishing I was with you...
Christmas is here - or is it? Does it have much feeling for you?
I miss the love so very much, yet I will never forget our faceless past...
So, I sit here and tears roll down my face,
Lord, is there no end to my disgrace?
I am not used to being alone, and I am so scared...
All I want is security, but I do not deserve it.
I suppose this means I still care,
I really don't want that.
I'd rather hate you and have a frozen heart.
Can't you see how much I was hurt,
Or my uncontrolled feelings of despise...
Can you see the love gone wrong
Mirrored in my tear-shined eyes?

(1990)

# FEBRUARY'S SILENT EMBRACE

The waves softly touching desert-like sands...
The sea gulls making known their demands...
The wind whispering through budded leaves...
The water rises as the snow grieves...
Familiar birds fly back home,
To ready their nests for the unborn.

Colors change from gray to green...
As the rain washes Earth's face clean.
The stars shine brighter than before...
As do the eyes of those who adore,
The glorious feelings from this wonderful place;
Brought by the tides of February's silent embrace.

(1990)
*Published 1999 Hardcover Anthology: *The Great Beyond* - National Library of Poetry
* Editor's Choice Award for Outstanding Achievement in Poetry
*Published 2002, by *Country Connection Magazine* as "Spring's Silent Embrace"
*Published 2005, by *Communicator Newsletter*

# DREAM MAN

Silent days...
And deadly nights.
Haunting memories...
The incredible yearning;
For some one new...
Someone to hold on to;
Someone who's honest, and true...
Who accepts me for who I am,
And cares for me;
(Without being overbearing)
Passionate...softly forceful...
A dream, if ever there was one.

(1990)

# GAME OF LOVE

Tears and heartache, and pain, and all,
Are just part of this treacherous game.
Insecurities, jealousy and control,
Are just weapons with a name.
This game is a serious one,
Where wonderful dreams of sweet romance,
Give power to schemes of deceit.

By now you should know the name,
Of this exciting, yet dangerous game,
Whose joy-filled moments of sweet romance,
Entice us to gamble again, and again.
Yet no matter which move a player makes,
Though the pieces may still separate;
The board is in continuous play.

(1990)
*Published 1998 in the Hardcover Anthology: *Beyond The Horizon* - National Library of Poetry
*Editor's Choice Award for Outstanding Achievement in Poetry

# TOGETHER YET APART

I am glad we are still friends,
That we can still relate;
I am glad we made amends,
Before it was too late.
Yes, we live our separate lives now.
'Cause time is too soon lost and gone,
But together -yet apart- we'll make it somehow.
We will be forever friends, this I now know.
No matter what comes, no matter what goes.
Together -yet apart- we will continually grow,
Until, together, we reach our highest goals.
Then, on that day, we will celebrate again,
What we have conquered together, my friend.
Helping each other, along the way,
We can make it through another day.

(1990) - Ode to Roxanne

# GO AHEAD AND CRY

You give love with all your heart,
Until you endure no more.
Now things start to fall apart,
You have used all you had in store.
The tears begin to fill the brim,
And you start to softly cry,
For bygone years and how they dim.

Long ago, when laughter came easy,
It was so simple to believe
In fairy tales, romance, and magic…
But now you can only grieve.
You ask what happened to that child,
Full of laughter and innocence.
Life then seemed so exciting and wild…
Until you were forced to learn defense.

I know that sometimes you want to run from life;
And sometimes you just can't be that strong.
Love and hate tangles you in strife.
So now, pour out your mournful song.
Cry now, for all those illusions that fooled,
And your wasted summer nights,
For because of them, your heart has cooled,
And become cynical, demanding rights.

(1990)

# GOING NOWHERE IN A HURRY

I want your crushing love,
Your painful arms.
I desire your thoughtless possession,
That could only harm.
I crave your hard words,
That set me on edge.
I need your cruel passion...
Oh, to be held in bed!
But I fool every one...
I keep on a smile.
And knowingly, I lie to them
All the while.
I am crying inside, yet...
I manage to keep deceiving.
But when I hear your name...
I begin to fall.
I begin to wonder if...
Anything matters to you at all.
I am falling in the rapids,
Through a vast open hole.
I am losing my sanity...
And lost all control.
Where am I going?
And what led to this end?

I only know how to hide,
To pretend and defend.
In ignorance,
I trudge to nowhere.
Going nowhere…
On a long, empty journey.
Going nowhere…
In a long, lonely hurry.

(1990)

# INNER PEACE

I let myself believe that it would be alright,
Though my mind stayed awake each and every night.
My thoughts are now so complicated.
And my dreams - fallen out of sight.
Some feeling I cannot explain,
Other than being jealous of an easy life,
And lover's foolish, yet compelling smiles.
Time is going by so fast,
(Should be against the law - a crime...)
Feelings of such loneliness, and aching confusion
Disturbs my inner peace.
Will this turmoil ever cease?
My hopes will rise, then are cruelly crushed...
Maybe I dream or want too much...
(Or maybe I just don't know enough...)
But must I bear alone this all?
Is this God's way of making me tough?
I feel so lost in this inner world of confusion,
With it's cold, soiled, marble walls...
(Am I fun... pretty... good... true?)
Yes, I worry too much, this I already know,
About trivial things and whether I'm in control.
Confusion... Hysteria...worry... ponder... wonder...
(...Fear...)
It is time stop this haunting inner disease...
Only I can tell it to cease...

(1990)

# JOY OF LIVING

That well-known feeling has come along again.
Burning forgotten scars; forgot they had ever been.
Anger and its fierce torments,
Fill my mind with utter anguish.
The used, abused, and torn in two...
A well worn mat too thin and frail.
I often wonder if it is worth it.
And if I will be able to pull through.
The injustice of it all,
Makes effort hard to emit.
There are so many goals to conquer,
So many dreams that could fail...
As I try to make them a reality, I wonder,
If it is easiest to give up.
No, the time for me to live is now.
Pick up the pieces and start the cruise.
Drop the chains and push off the dock,
Joy in my life, is yet to come.

(1990)

## MUSIC FEEDS MY SOUL

Beyond all the pain and tortures of love,
A peaceful harmony rises above…
A song so soothing - yet vengeful, alike;
A song of such emotion, can make it seem alright.
When I'm feeling down - either high, or out of control,
I hide deep inside the songs and the music feeds my soul.

(1990)

## MY THANKS TO YOU

My thanks to you, my friend,
For everything that you do.
And ever standing by me -
Though I can be such a fool.
I am never ashamed to reveal,
Those things I really feel
For I can rely on you.
So my thanks to you, again,
My sweet enduring friend -
For everything you do,
And accepting me as I am.

(1990)

# NOT SO NONCHALANT

Listening to the late night news,
Flipping through all the channels;
Trying to feel amused,
And shake that old familiar feeling.
Of being walked on…
…Of being used.
Wishing my heart could be thrown away
Like a burned out fuse
That was too often abused.
But can it, will it ever burn again;
And do I really want it to?

(1990)

# AS THE SECONDS TICK ON BY

...One... Two...Three... Four...
Someone's knocking at my rusty door,
He's standing there, patiently he waits.
Tell me why I still hesitate...
...Nine... Ten... Eleven...Twelve...
Inside me, restless fear dwells.
As the seconds tick on by,
Flying fast - so precious, so dear.
...Thirteen... Fourteen... Fifteen, now...
I would turn the knob if I only knew how.
Will I ponder ever more?
Will my feet cross the forbidden floor?
Quickly went Nineteen -and Twenty followed...
What if I find my heart's been hollowed?
Awkwardly - my hand reaches, timidly...
Only to fall at the sight of humility.
For no one waits outside my door...
No one craves my love any more...
Next time - I swear to myself,
I will not hesitate,
When next I hear that opening of my gate.

(1990)

# SILENT UNWELCOMING HOME

Why must I be alone?
To walk amidst an echoed home?
Where no one waits in my empty bed,
And no one hears what I have said.
How many tears must I cry?
I feed myself unhealthy lies,
Which have no beginning - or an end.
A meaningless life becomes a game of pretend.
What will the future hold?
Where will I be when I grow old?
Alone and cold, without a sound.
Why must I always say I can?
When what I need is a solid man?
Will I ever find someone?
Who will be there when my time is done?
How many heartaches must I endure.
Before I find the one who will be secure?
No matter how full, how busy, how cluttered –
It remains a silent, unwecloming home.

(1990)

# FLY AWAY!

Fly…
Be on your way,
Spread your wings and soar.
Do not waste time and delay.
Do what is needed for you.
Stock your soul with satisfaction.
And fulfill your desires.
But once you've sung your song,
And your wings are bruised and sore,
Remember from whence you've come.
Walk on home to me, my friends,
And I'll do my best to comfort you.
While you rest and mend.
And when you are well enough to fly again,
After you, my love I will send,
To help you make your stand.
I will be waiting for your return,
With soft bandages and a welcoming hand.

(1990)

# I CARE!

Who are you to disturb my inner thoughts?
To come here, innocently driving my fears away;
Creating new fears… as the old ones fade?
Don't go - but for God's sake don't stay.
Show yourself to me… or just go away.
Your feelings are welcome here… I think,
Wanting your smiles and tears;
And with you, I lose some fear.
Yet I try not to care.
I may not be able to stop the flow.
Gotta ask you to stop this… but please don't you go.
I am confused between my fears and you
To you, I am who I am.
Still you stay where you stand.
I fear I may enjoy this too much…
Might not let go of your hand.
I'll be strong, take it as it comes… Enjoy our time.
Wait for the inevitable chime.
I'll try not to push you away, I swear.
Nor will I show you too much.
Yet it is so hard not to believe in this…

(1990)- Ode to Dave

# I WILL PREVAIL

There's knowledge in abundance, all around.
Seems to be easily tripped over and found.
Yet just can't seem to get enough:
To get anywhere seems so very tough.
Just have to reach out and grab it...
Have to make positive attitude a habit.
Wanna do so very much...
Just desire the winner's touch.
So very impatient... in a hurry,
And let myself too often worry.
Suppose, in time, it will all come.
Pray it happens, before my time has gone.
Life's crazy humor of surprise,
Teaching me to fairly compromise.
Try to do the best I can,
And keep from following every day men.
Will do whatever I think is best
And if I fail, will I still pass the test?
My goal is to love and to learn,
To accomplish what I now yearn,
To leave my footprints on life's crazy trail,
And against all else, I will prevail.

(1990)

# INFATUATION IN RESERVE

Infatuated, I steal a glance.
No eye contact is allowed.
So, quickly… look away,
And shake off that daydream romance!
It's been a century or two, since I've felt this way…
So, forgive me as confusion stumbles my speech,
And lost, I forget what I had to say;
Though I had rehearsed those lines so well.
But someday I'll get the nerve,
And in confidence, I'll smile.
Yet the reason I remain so stone cold silent,
Is that by you, I could be hurt.
And this potential danger frightens me,
For I know how it feels to be burned.
So, for now I'll reserve my infatuation,
Until this feeling goes away.
For the part of me that could learn to care,
Can easily be shoved away!

(1990)

# LOST AND CONFUSED

I can't go on like this,
Thinking of what I've missed…
And blaming those who could have given
A more stable life, a better life.
Can't dwell on being alone;
But there is nothing else I've known.
The love of someone, a friend.
These things I don't see, because I don't share.
I've become so good at a game called pretend…
That I don't know what's real any more.
I often feel frustrated because no one sees this;
And because I can't seem to get life right.
People are so hard to understand and like.
And traditional values blind my flight.
I'm lost and confused,
In a rotting world.
I'm feeling so small…
Like a forgotten little girl…
A bad girl - a banished girl.

(1990)

# MIRROR TALK

You are not too bad;
You try to take care of yourself,
Though it's in a lazy way.
You laugh a lot, and keep on a cheer;
Though it's only to hide,
Your deepest shadowed fears.
You cry a lot, and dwell on your faults,
But you try to give credit,
When you pull through it all.
Though you are always confused,
And worry on trivial things,
You know what you want.
And you are not getting it here.
You try to be liked - maybe too hard.
And you're semi-conscience of appearance.
You are softhearted,
And find it hard to let anyone down.
You would rather trust than not;
Even when the time has worn through.
You don't open up enough,
And you keep thoughts in tight.
Yet you are loyal and kind…
And you are always a winner,
As long as you try.

(1990)

# Months

5 months of emotions
And bitter tearful pain
5 months of learning
And partied nights in vain
5 months gone by
8 - since the break-up
And finally doors have opened
Letting fresh air in again

(1990)

# ON MY OWN, I'VE GROWN

While I sit here, drinking my coffee,
I think of you again, my eternally haunting friend.
Will the love I held ever end,
Instead of slowly receding, to the back of my mind?
Slightly shrinking away, each and every day.
I think about how you changed your ground,
Before we parted,
And now I wonder what would've happened,
If I stuck around,
Would I still be broken hearted?
I've grown a lot - and done a lot.
And through it all, alone.
Though I still think of you,
I refrain from letting it be known.
My life is my own, now,
I know I will make it somehow.
I don't need, nor depend on you,
I depend on me.
Feeling that is so very freeing.
I no longer cry over you,
I never feel your pain.
I no longer shake when I hear your name.
And when I think of your primitive game,
How it has left you…
I know you never wanted me to go,
But oh, how I have learned to grow!
Live education - on my own.
And I think, because of this,
You, too, have grown.

(1990) – Ode to Darcy

# MUTUAL INFATUATION

So you've spoken out now;
Said what you had on your mind.
But don't you see,
Just what your words have done to me?
Now that the words have been spoken,
What are we to do with them?
Just wait for the demeaning end?
You started the flirtation and opened the doors...
Yet there are obstacles in every corridor.
Just what do you mean by the things that you say?
...Yet now we stay quiet and distant...
With our mutual infatuation.
Strange how such sharing
Can create such an uncomfortable barrier.

(1990) - Ode to Dave, my loving husband.

# MY DOOR - EVERMORE

Soft, shallow music flowing,
Birds whispering their quiet, undemanding love,
Lustrous trees bending to the powerful wind...
That's just outside my door - evermore.
Can't you hear the music from where you stand?
The echoed chirps of love?
Can you feel the wind blowing, my friend?
Just outside my open door – evermore.
Inside the open door...
Is a small, neat, cozy mat.
And on its face clearly written: *welcome*.
To your right is a place for your hat.
Inside my door - evermore.
Yes, I've been hurt, and burned, and stepped on too.
And even cried tears, just like you.
You are safe inside my door.
Look - open your eyes and see.
No pressure, no pain, no cutting words.
Things to be left in the outside world.
Look again - my friend,
No accusations, no consolations.
Only fascination in what you have to say.
We can talk or sit in silence; inside my open door.
We can love, lust, or like - whichever you prefer.

But in honesty, my friend - evermore.
My door opens to a sanctuary that I built alone, in full control.
And no matter where I live, or how,
It always holds on to part of my soul.
Inside my door, it's so damn easy to give.
And inside my door, life isn't so hard to live - anymore.
So come on in, step inside the door.
When you are ready, it will be held in store.
My door is open, for you - evermore...

(1990)

# PAIN

Today I cried...
Bearing all my pain...
Forming puddles in vain.
Wishing it all away;
To be able to enjoy,
And not be afraid.
Today I cried,
And yesterday as well...
But now my eyes are aching,
And have begun to swell...
Becoming empty voids of confusion;
Getting harder and colder with each passing night.
Tell me what's the use of crying?
And what's the use of pain?
When every day seems to bring the same;
Just vicious circles of unaccountable shame!

(1990)

# PEOPLE'S TALK

Disappointed, once again...
I hover over my well-used pen.
Trying hard to think of words,
To explain how I really feel.
How people's words so often allure.
They repeat some of what they hear,
And part of what they choose to see;
Then they add whatever they fear.
People talk and people walk,
Down the same well beaten paths.
Am I the only one this shocks?
Aren't we here to learn to love...
To learn to ride this earth,
Without this need to push and shove?
Yet we clamor all over each other...
Shouting out false words, purposely hurting one another.
We care not where we step, or on who...
A simpleton race, remaining faithfully unkind - untrue.

(1990)

# SMILE, BE HAPPY!

Smile - be happy!
It's time to get things snappy!
You're off to the bar,
But from there you won't get far…
And you will pay for it tomorrow!
Yet while you are in the bar,
You will feel like a star…
Burning distinctively bright.
But you won't remember much tomorrow.
And tomorrow doesn't change.
And life remains just as strange.
So this attempt to cover,
Did nothing, but discover,
That the bar wasn't really worth it after all!

(1990)

# THE DAY AFTER

Surprise...Surprise...
No mysteries, no disguise,
Nothing but honesty enhanced,
In our communal eyes.
No complicated lies,
No faces, only transparent panels;
Used only for protection - got to survive.
That is the way we live our human lives.
The passion we shared kept me smiling throughout the day.
Frustrations that always follow the dawn,
Were so easily washed away.
Thank God, there's no misunderstanding,
There's no pride - only caution,
To prevent experiencing pain.
So much to lose - so very much to gain...
Burning flame; physical desire...
Red hot! To touch is to scorch!
Better be careful, my sweet, sweet man,
For you may have lit my rained on torch...
A feat few could manage.
Gone today, here tomorrow - and after, we don't know
No plans - no demands...
Just here, tonight, now.
Hold me... touch me... just like before.
Don't stop, now that you've started.
But if you must leave, now would be better;
For, now won't leave me broken-hearted.

(1990) - Ode to Dave, my loving husband

# THE GIFT OF MUSIC

Quiet…
Silence…
Subtle calmness fills the air.
Wisps of softly played music flows…
As vocals join on time to share,
A harmonized joy that one very rarely knows.
Listen…
Relax…
Pull up a cozy chair.
Dream along with the music now,
Let it carry you there,
Amid the pleasures of its sound.
Enjoy…
Relish…
Spend some time with yourself.
Listen to the words in earnest.
Soak in the treasured wealth,
For this is your time for mental health.
Cry…
Laugh…
Let it all go.
You can show yourself here, now.
And let yourself grow.
This is the gift that music brings.
Holding its special moments in store.
And as long as you relish in what it sings,
Life lightens and is no longer such a chore.

(1990)

# ONE AND ONLY ME

People say I am fine as I am,
No need to think of changes,
To find virtues, if I can.
But this becomes deranged.
I can't say I'm single...anymore
And I'm not sure I consider that good.
Yet I have full control over my feelings (I think),
And over all else,
I'm not about to change my ways.
Been doing them far too long.
Sometimes I wonder if improvements would only enhance,
All other wrongs I do, by chance.
But people just have to except me,
No bright colors, no make-up, no pizzazz.
Only what you see,
The original one and only me.
I do wish I was more exciting,
That I had interesting things to say…
…more fit, healthier, prettier.
But those things are only colors.
Not included in my aura's gray.
So here I am…
Just me, myself and I.
Virtues, faults and all,
Not willing to color myself with dyes.

(1990)

# SOMETIMES I FEEL

Sometimes, I feel like I'm lost in a crowd,
And there's nothing but darkness, all around.
Sometimes, I feel like a whirlwind went by,
Leaving me breathless and tossed - wondering why.
Sometimes, I want to run to another land,
And start a new life there - if I can.
Sometimes, I wonder if I have done all I can.
There are many roads that call out demands.
Sometimes, I feel that it will only take time,
A few more months, and it will be fine.
And sometimes, I feel I can do anything,
Feel oblivious to the pain life so often brings.
Sometimes, I don't wonder, or feel at all…
And those are the times I take the hardest fall.

(1990)

# TIME FOR ME, MYSELF AND I

Black on black,
And splashes of light.
Glowing... Shining...
Silently winking at night.
Looking at the darkened sky,
Gazing at the hazy moon,
Dreaming of another place.
Hoping I get there soon.
So peaceful, so quiet...
Out here, alone.
No shouting, no arguments.
No ringing of a phone.
Time now for quiet thought.
Nature...and myself,
Time so carefully bought.
Time to put the world on a dusty shelf.
Not a sound out here tonight,
Just the creatures of the night...
Just me, myself and I...
And the peaceful darkened sky.

(1990)

# SURVIVOR

Here I am again,
Writing down feelings with my near-dry pen.
Yet I am not really sure,
What words I should use to begin.
Things are looking up.
Life is not so tough, anymore.
Getting easier and easier,
To walk out my door.
I have finally seen some results,
From my efforts, pain and turmoil...
I never have to go through them again.
I will be all right,
I will make it okay.
Suddenly I have the strength,
To make it another day.
I know I will survive.
I can be truly alive.
And won't ever feel like before,
I have a firm hand on a solid shore.
This time, it will be done right.
Keeping my goals clearly in sight,
For now that I have learned to decipher,
Between which steps to take, and how high,
I am learning when to risk a stake...
And feel the victory of a survivor!

(1990)

# THE MOMENT

The moment is near,
The slightly haunting moment,
I have wanted to have for years.
This moment is now here.
So why am I so frightened?
So scared inside?
Why does my mind circle and storm?
Why do my legs try to run - my body hide?
I do not want to remain here,
This moment can take me away.
Yet now that this moment is near,
I feel no excitement, just fear.

(1990)

# THE WOMAN IS ME

Sedated mind
Solitary heart
Feeling lost, yet strangely in control
Riding hard
Risking near to none
Raising doubtful brows
Remaining determinedly young
Steady as she grows
Learning as she goes
Trying, falling, getting up again
Facing her detested foes
Reacting on hate, and love
Nothing in between
Often wanting to give up
But she has a long way to go
And she loves the challenge, I know
Forever; her dream - her goal
This woman I know very well
Together, we been back and forth from hell
And to pastures that seemed more green
Yet only alone, behind closed doors
Only in my mirror, is she seen.

(1990)

# WALKING SHOES

Something came up,
And shadowed my hopes, again.
Are my dreams really so demanding?
I am young - still learning the ropes.
Can't find my inspirations,
They have fallen out of sight…
Seem to dissipate with gaining speed.
Find it hard to stick to what is right.
Working hard to obtain what I know I'm worth;
While others work towards nothing.
And obstacles keep sprouting up,
From the cold - heartless Earth.
Thinking of where I should be…
…of what I could be.
Trying to keep in sight what I know is good for me.
While craving only the worst paths.
I don't know an awful lot,
But I know what hurts can't be right.
As I slip and slide down my chosen paths,
I just want to get high…
Here's to hoping I learn quick,
And do what ever it is I need to do,
So I won't always work so hard…
While I wear these walking shoes.

(1990)

# WHAT'S BOTHERING ME?

Blank mind, this time.
An empty space - a vacant room.
A hollowed out cave, echoing darkness and gloom.
Don't feel lonely, or lost in the rain.
Don't feel anger - just a haunting pain…
Tears no longer roll down my face and stain,
For I know the dawn's about to shine…
It will only take a little more time.
I'm almost there - so close to where I want to be.
The solution to my problems, I can clearly see.
Walking up the steep path, now slightly descending…
So what is it that is bothering me?
I lay here, drowning myself in bubbly wine,
Trying to escape… what? …I don't know.
Too much calmness inside.
Waters turned to a glassy calm - no longer raging wild.
Can't seem to sum up, what's bringing me down.
What is it that caused this constant frown?
My eyes too swollen to see through the clouds;
Can't figure out what's bothering me.

(1990)

# WORDS

Vocabulary on a wheel...
Mumbled words spat out in a spiel,
Yet very rarely are they real.
Understated... over-mused...
Is it comprehension - or compromise?
Better hope they're big enough in size!
So often stated,
That they're underrated.
And so, false meanings are then created.
Try to sound sincere...
Yet holding back words in fear,
From being too often jeered.
So many sums lead to so many substances.
Hard to force yourself to take the chances,
And all hell breaks loose if there's wrong glances.
Despite it all the truth is not truly heard.
Because of the wrong combinations of words...
An ironic wheel of confusion is needlessly churned.

(1990)

# A SURENESS ON THIS SUMMER NIGHT

Cool - silent.
Naught a sound.
Save the softly played music,
And the fan spinning,
Round and round.
Peace - calm.
Nothing moving,
Save the moon,
So beautiful tonight, such stamina…
Her soft light filling earth's panorama.
Feel's so heavenly right,
On this sedating night.
Alone - I sorted my thoughts,
Have them straight once again.
Try not to fall off track,
Can't remember feeling so calm, so high.
Not excited - just determined.
Not shy - just taking it slow.
Finally feeling close to me;
This flighty sparrow.
There's a feeling here so right.
A sureness on this summer night.

(1990)

# ALWAYS, TO YOU - MY UNDYING THOUGHTS I SEND.

Strange, how it happened;
The ability to love again.
Never thought the last one would end.
And now it's happened again.
I am feeling stronger, this time.
Yet slightly vulnerable, inside.
Still, some of our love I dutifully hide,
To keep, for me - always close by my side.
I thought of you, just before I let you go.
Felt sorrowful, in a way.
The thought rushed by - didn't stay.
His love pushed it away.
He showed me all I have ever craved.
Holds me close - protecting.
Gently secure - never rejecting.
In his hands - skillfully saved.
Once, we shared a love, at first, then tears.
Time has sadly separated you and I.
And now - I love again.
Nothing to lose, I never lost before.
...Just had to let you know...
I've finally let you go;
But I will always care.
How you do and how you fare.
One day we will meet again...
I'd like you to meet him then.
To you - my undying thoughts I send.

(June 25, 1990) – Ode to Darcy

# WITHOUT RESTRAINING BARS:

What words can I say, my love?
What phrase should I use?
How can I describe this glow,
Without leaving you confused?
I cannot say the words, I know.
They might make you run.
I don't want to push you away,
And these words only load the gun.
Should I remain silent, my dear?
And hold these words deep, yet near?
Will you run, if I let them go?
They hold such dangers, I know.
I will do whatever it takes to see you smile,
Even if it means letting you go.
I will be supportive, my love, all the while.
No domination, no type of controls.
I'll never hold on tight, nor will I let you slip away.
Giving you room to choose your own way.
I will never betray your trust in me,
I only hope you choose to stay.
Hold my hand, walk beside me - I pray,
And we'll travel to a distant burning star.
Yes, my love, I will be hurt if you stray too far,
But I love you, David,
Without restraining bars.

(June 12, 1990) - Ode to Dave

# CONSPIRACY

Conspiracy lies
Just beneath
Those shaded eyes.
Pretty face,
All dressed in lace,
In it for power's taste.
Costing jobs
People's happiness...
People's homes...
Leaving their dreams wasted.
Burn the people,
While their children hunger.
Age creeps up,
You are not getting younger.
Step softly and you will be trusted.
Step hard and you have corrupted.

(1990)

# LOVE IS NEVER A MISTAKE

Carried away with the flow of raining tears
Falling out of darkened skies.
Occasional sounds of thunder,
Trying to raise the child's fears.
Watching as the world turns a brilliant green,
Sparkling from wetted leaves.
Smelling, now, so fresh and clean.
Another wonder went by unnoticed.
Sounds from the radio tell a story,
Over and over - you know it well.
Telling of a broken heart full of pain,
And the vow to never care again.
Don't they see that love is never a mistake?
That it is good to feel again?
And to never love,
Would be to live a life in vain.

(1990)

# MY MIDNIGHT VOW

Another day - another dollar,
One more inch, and I'd be taller.
Within my reach,
Just around the corner.
I have to hang on.
Survive a little longer.
Got to be strong...
Can't afford more tears,
Wasted, that way, so many years.
Could have been there yesterday...
Got to concentrate on today.
Can't waste my tomorrows,
Thinking on yesterday's sorrows.
Wonder if I can make it there...
Yet can't afford to let myself care.
Will get there as soon as I can.
Won't wait for no one else, no-how!
Can't afford more time now.

(1990)

# LOVE OF A MANY FACE

Love of a many face,
I shy from your disgrace.
Love of a many hill,
I won't let go of my will.
Tumbling, falling…
Just tired of stalling.
Can't let it fade away,
Yet won't allow myself to beg.
My heart means so much more.
Yes, I step harder...than before.
Why jump blinded, headfirst,
Into the never ending thirst.
Slowly, I watch and sigh.
Silently, I smother my cries.
Trying to hold onto what, I don't know.
But never - no never, let it show.
My eyes see danger up ahead.
Threatening to leave my heart stone dead.
Tonight, I caress my greatest fear.
To love you always, and hold you near.

(1991)

# MY CHILD

I dream, of someone, somewhere.
To hold her, my child.
I dream of how she sounds,
How she cries…
Would she find out her mother's lies?
Could she be proud of me,
And the life I lead?
She calls me some nights,
And haunted, I dream…
I hear her wordless voice.
Call to me, reaching in fright.
I can't reach her, try as I might.
Screaming she falls from my sight!
I stare, hearing her wordless voice,
Echoing in the night.

(1991)
* The child is a little girl from my past… me.

# EDUCATED LIES

I grieve for this world, as it fights its wars,
Where humans all slam their doors.
Here, people starve, knowing only pain.
While others, rich, stake out their claim.
Sad to see... such emptiness I feel.
This world cannot last forever;
Life's just a one time deal.
Man, thinking ourselves unbeatable,
Tried to conquer with knowledge we lacked.
Now, so far destroyed, Earth takes her final stance,
While we pray for just one second chance.
We watch, knowing what our children will see.
Helpless, we cannot undo this awful disease.
So watch, my people, my educated men,
Just watch your ancestors' victory descend.
While you sit at your desks and thunder your speeches,
Cry, for your child's child will live to die,
Because of educated men - educated to lie.

(1991)

# A LONG TIME AGO

I am thinking of a time,
A long time ago.
When I was with you,
A long time ago.
A song plays, and your words fly home,
From a long, long time ago.
When you had many a bed traveled,
And many more to go.
I have had a hard time since then,
Finding out who I am, and why we ran.
Being alone - our child unborn.
Facing life, I have grown since that day,
A long time ago.
Yet I still feel and hurt.
Ashamed of my shell,
I hide in hell - afraid of being weak.
Those years caused it so,
Such a long, long time ago.
Trying to feel good - like I know I should.
And when I do feel good,
I will leave that day,
From a long time ago,
Far, far away.

(1991)

## INSIGNIFICANT

Sometimes I feel like such a child,
Small, insignificant, afraid and mild.
Don't see the reasons for my life...
Don't see the reasons for this pain.
Hate making so many mistakes.
Afraid of taking a higher risk.
Clinging to what securities I can hold.
Worried I will, or won't, succeed.
Inner battles, galore...
Though, some how, I'm gaining momentum,
More and more.

(1991)

# FEBRUARY NINTH

A man I once knew,
Lies now unable to hear.
No one there to hold his hand,
To lessen his fear.
They won't let me in,
For I'm not his kin.
So in thought, I worry, I bleed for his need.
A woman I know,
Slowly Dies…
Unashamed, she cries.
I hold her dear.
Yet hide in fear,
Of her death,
Slowly taking her away from me.
Shameful avoidance.
So I sit here drinking my tea,
Not tasting a thing.
Craving for a smoke,
Or better yet a toke.
For I cannot handle it alone.
Tired, I pray to hear steps…
And hearing none,
I go to find a smoke.

(1991)

# ME AND YOU

I anticipate your call…
I follow the lights, as they pass,
Only to find, it's not you - alas!
I wonder what could keep you.
What keeps you away from me?
I reach, I call, and you are not there.
On my knees, I beg you to show you care.
A token, a wink, a touch…
Yet you do not hear my unspoken plea.
Dutifully, I patiently wait
For you to find time,
Time to decide our fate.

Never barking a claim,
Never do I complain,
Trying to give whatever it takes.
But honey, I hurt when you don't call.
Tears well, and gritty feelings grind.
Afraid, I drown my tears in wine.
A voice whispers, "wasting time."
Yet I wait here - giving room.
Hoping you need it too.
Do I build this up to be more than it is?
Yet I feel everything in your solitary kiss.
And I wait - following every light, as they pass by.

(1991)

# MISSING HER

Sharing very little,
Pretending it's less,
Only to get and there suggest,
That I have gotten in a mess.
I gave more than I was willing,
Now, my heart is chilling,
I must go find the girl.
I left behind a pearl,
All over a nagging fear.

(1990)

# ON LIFE

Dream for the sky,
The true blue high.
Looking down,
You will ever ask why,
The world is, as it is.
See the people, the little people,
Hiding behind a false steeple,
Pretending to be what they are not.
I hear people speak,
Of the world they seek,
Found only in books they themselves wrote.
There is no hero.
No one to wipe your sorry ass.
Turning our backs on our pasts,
We do over what was done before.
While our people sit and speak,
Of the happiness we all seek,
And upon finding it…
…turn and spit.
In greed, we strike, and strike again.
Our sad need for more.
And in my simple way,
I stumble, looking for truth.
Confused - I look again,
And there I see a long-lost friend,
Ready to begin my teaching.
Just the start of a long tending…

(1991)

# PAINFUL CHOICE

Can anyone hear my worthless plea?
To support me, and let me be?
Can anyone help me through this maze?
I feel locked in a wired cage.
One false move will set the trap,
And my overloaded heart will snap.
I would cry, if I could.
But I am not sure I should.
With so much to choose,
And so very much to lose.
To decide what I want more, now,
Without losing somehow.
It's a failing gain.
STOP!
I am going insane!
My love has changed my life to his.
My time no longer my own,
My friends - abandoned,
Moved on.
And because I choose to love,
I have also chosen to lose.

(1991)

# POINTLESSNESS

Tired, I watch my heart
Beat a little slower,
Sink a little lower.
Feeling, so much - yet so little,
Automatic shut-down
Heart-break bound.
Anger can be so cold
Solid, like a rock,
A sharp shock.
Sorrow, fills my pointless corpse
With stinking dismay.
Without delay,
I refuse to see what I have seen before,
It's just not worth it any more.
Just to try now, seems such a chore
Would rather let it go…

(1990)

# RAPTURE

Today you angered,
And I stood aside,
Ready to duck and hide.
But in time, you smiled.
You never raised a hand,
Nor spoke a hard command.
Just a problem you faced in stride,
And I think I loved you more.

(1990) – Ode to Dave, a sweet and patient man.

# SHADOW

A shadow slithers by.
The child wonders why,
...just as I.
Alone - yet surrounded.
Confused and astounded,
As the shadow slithers 'round.
Only permitting a glimpse,
So damn easy to dismiss;
'Til it shows again.
Try to hide it now,
Yet I am not sure how,
To set it right.
So instead, I fight.
Wanted more yesterday,
Opportunity missed today.
I just cannot find my way.
So, lost, I forget to feel.
And the shadow slithers by,
Without ever revealing why,
It sneaks around.

(1990)

# SILENT YEARNING

How can I lay here silent,
Never really saying what is meant?
Stubborn, I hold onto a tear.
Afraid to loose - my tongue is mute;
I feel nothing on the subjects
Of which I say nothing.
Feeling frozen and hating it.
I hear women speak,
Of this thing I desire,
Yet no feeling of it,
Has inspired,
My coldness away.
Feeling foolish
For faking it.
My hopes dissipate
With every moon.
When this feeling arises,
Shadowed, it comes out;
With every moon a new face
While I stand dumbfounded.

(1991)

# ODE TO VINCE

Those times in our growing years,
Those nights of so many tears,
You were my friend and we played in the clubhouse.
There we drank and told tales…
We've partied like young, giddy children do.
You liked me, and I knew.
Years later we "went out," - your chance to ask.
I was vulnerable and lonely;
And I hurt you.
We met again, years later…another place.
As roommates…buddies…lovers.
Things went wrong once again,
A confusion of friendship and need.
And now to look in your eyes again…
You seem much the same;
Yet I feel uncomfortable this time.
The flame you held for so long has died.
And I felt its presence gone.
I hope you have forgiven me for my mistakes,
My inadequacies in communication.
Please understand that I was a broken, violated child.
And I have been stumbling since the age of four.
Did you ever know of the men in my childhood?
How I became their target?

I've never understood men's sexual sides…let alone my own.
Please understand that never in my darkest moment,
Did I want to hurt you.
Though I know I have so many times
…as I have others.
Afraid of being rejected, of being a freak,
Of deserving what I got.
Never knowing where the boundaries lay.
And with that I denied everything.
This note, one long overdue…
Is to express the sorrow I feel.
Know that I have always treasured
The precious part you have played in my life,
And value the friendship we shared.

(1991)

# THANK YOU, MY FRIEND

Thank you, my friend,
For coming here.
Just having you near,
When I needed you most.
I had so much to say,
We rattled on and on,
Never slowing.
I just had to let you know,
Just telling you,
Helped me to decide,
Without you saying a word,
Just the fact you really heard.
And now I sit, relieved,
Because you listened,
While I grieved.

(1991)

# WHAT A WASTE

I don't want to get use to not having you there,
After all this time, it just isn't fair.
Such a waste can leave such a bitter taste.
I don't want to get use to being alone, again.
How can you look at me and say you don't understand?
How can you treat it as though it laid light in your hand?
Hell, that's just fine - after all this wonderful time!
We ought not to make conclusions with such haste.
Just to give up so easily - just letting go.
Without letting this settle in until we know.
I am too damn afraid to play this game,
Where everyone designates the blame.
I wait for you to follow through,
With what you once said you would do.
But to let go before we've even tasted,
Seems to me, to be time truly wasted.

(1990)

# A THOUGHT

Most of us are mixed of heart.
Most of us have been torn apart.
How much pain can one endure,
And still retain some innocence?
Is it just me, or do others see,
This comical, sadistic error of confusion
That we are pleased to call human.

(1991)

# CAREFUL NOW!

Just what is it you want me to say?
That I'm scared and want to run away?
That I don't know if I'm strong enough?
That I'm tired of trying to feel another way?
So there you are - the words in dark pen.
Tell me, please, what are you gonna do with them?
Can you stand beside me still and again?
Or should I walk, forget about talk,
And travel to where I've often been.
I don't want to go -"rejection"
Crying all day over nothing of worth.
Feeling the pain of a long ago adventure...
What's wrong with being careful?
Of looking after me first?

(1991)

# I LOVE YOU THAT MUCH

Can you hear the fan blowing
Trying in vain to cool
On this hot summer day?
Holding you close, so strong
Feels as though nothing
Will ever go wrong.
I part the hairs on your chest
Just to feel them curl around my finger
Like a chick cuddled in her nest.
Your eyes bathe me in their embrace.
And it feels so good for it to be this way
New and exciting in the same
Knowing that it is here to stay.
I have felt so inadequate
Yet you seem to be fulfilled.
I only hope I can fill your need
I love you that much.

(1991)

# SHOW ME

Show me my tomorrow,
To ease today's sorrows,
And give me reason to believe
It will work out all right.
My dreams are uneasy tonight.
Show me my tomorrow,
So I know which road to follow,
And ease my dismay,
So I can sleep today.

(1991)

# THE SOUL WHISPERS

Can you hear the silent whispers of my soul,
As I reach out and take control,
Slipping out as I walk towards my goal?
Can you see the shine hidden in my eyes,
As I slowly let go of so many lies?
Got tired of letting them rule my life.
Do you hear the small child mourn her loss,
For all the people she's loved and lost?
Crying her fear of never coming rightly across?
Can you see the frown of fear,
Hidden by a face that I hold very dear?
Frightened to be alone, and of someone getting to near.
Are you able to hear the thoughts, never said?

(1991)

# THE SOUND OF A SOUL

Have you heard the sound of a soul set free?
The soul has many sounds,
And if you could hear them you'd agree.
But the only sounds a mortal hears,
Are the bitterness and the tears…
The sounds of blame, fear and shame.
But if you can, listen
Listen close, and hear
The harmonious singing…
The beautiful sound ringing
From that same soul, once masked and held prisoner
In the body you knew so long ago.
Yes the body has been asked to leave,
And it is alright to hurt and grieve.
Just listen closer and you'll hear,
That her soul is happier being free.

(1991)

# WIND

Wind is invisible - you cannot see it,
Yet you know it is there.
The movement of the trees and the grass,
And the movement through your hair.
Wind can never hurt you, never fear.
But it can cause things to hit you.
And when strong enough it moves
With incredible strength.
Yet in reality, physically, it is nothing.

Gossip: like wind, cannot hurt you in itself,
It can move others - if it is strong enough,
It can be uncontrollable and unpredictable…
Yet in reality, physically, it is nothing.

(1991)

# DESTINY

The leaves are falling down,
...down.
And the ground is cold,
...frozen.
Starting my life,
...I begin.
Trying hard to conquer,
...to win.
Feeling scared,
Sometimes weary.
Come home frustrated,
...and teary.
A calling - a yearning,
Is urging.
Mind regrets - ignores,
...purging.
Can I trust what I see?
What a charm to believe.
No matter what,
...I'll go.
A forbidding place,
...the unknown.

(1991)

# YOU

My heart warms when I touch you,
My eyes swarm with my love for you
And flows through my veins
It feels so good to know you are there.
I'm able to rely on you because you care.
Laughter tickles my very bones…
Leaving me happy, alive, and aware.
Tell me your every thought, no fear
I will tell you mine my dear.
Hold my hand - stand by my side.
From you, I have little to hide.
Just had to let you know,
The love I feel and how it's grown.
So, darlin', thanks for loving me,
And letting me - be me.

(1991) - my darling Dave

# WHAT TORE OUR FAMILY APART?

Production...
Constructive use of time...
Never able to enjoy being a child...
Never in classes or allowed to be wild....
My time was spent in a stupefied wonder.
I wanted to play, as a child, to laugh.
I wanted to sing and join groups.
Until, so criticized by myself,
My playfulness drooped.
Push, Push, Pushing
Act older, do more, grow up soon.
Feeling awkward and clumsy...
With the oncoming doom.
And now I punish myself
Echoing the reinforcement of my youth.
Stumbling, I am never good enough.
And in a stupor I passively wait.
Waiting for her to admit to her demands...
Her strict and painful ways of denial...
Her bitterness becoming our own...
Pushing us so far apart.

(1991)

# A THOUGHT OF LOSS

How will you deal with it?
Do you leave - will you run?
Two years coming soon,
And it's no longer just fun.
Some days are glorious,
And others - just routine.
Play your part, I'll play mine.
And we'll both pretend it will suffice.

(1992)

# A Contemplative Meditation

Fear...
Will he return to do me harm?
Will I walk innocently into him one day?
Fears rise up and swarm,
Enclosing me in a victim's cage.
No longer restrained by law,
Will he take his chance now, or wait?
I will not let it happen!
He would die! This I vow.
He has no strength against an adult.
He has no control over me - anymore.
I will not shrink away.
I am stronger than before.

It has happened, again.
Locked in a room today
With an obscene man.
Felt a chill of fear, a child again,
Why? I don't understand why.
I told this time, and he left,
No longer in control, he lied...
Such silly see-through lies.
I am glad there were others he victimized.
I hate always being the only one.
And why? I guess I will never know.

(1992) – Written after two traumatic events within a week of each other. The first was when a restraining order had expired, and the other was regarding indecent exposure.

# DOORS

I had always thought the world was so cruel,
Never realizing I have always shut, and opened my own doors.
Fears, reservations; past or present experiences; paranoia…

Have all twisted my fate,
And I succumbed to it.
I now know all experiences, good or bad;
Whether I considered them failures or accomplishments,
Have been learning experiences… lessons.

I have soul searched for several years,
Always growing; creating a yearning to grow more.
All those faces, curtains dropping down with each experience;
Learned ways of dealing with life,
Separating me from it.
Choices; opportunities influenced by emotions…
I don't want to live carrying baggage,
Or leave too many doors unopened.

(1992)
*Published 2004 in the Hardcover Anthology: *On the Wings of Poetry*

# FACING IT

Wanting a soul to lean on,
And a heart to hold.
Dare me to fly, it's my way…
Though I may stutter and fall.
I always feel so old.
So torn and so scared.
Kindness has made its way,
Wrapping me in a pretty,
Yet fragile shell.
Such fear unfolds.
Could not walk away.
I am here, shaking,
Auburn hair turned gray.
Scared of being alone.
Somehow found myself attached,
And have no need to break away.
Clinging, I hope I will be okay.
A man, friend, and my strength.
So glad it happened this way.
But can he ever know,
How very weak and fragile I am?
So very willing to believe…
Afraid I will spend my life forgetting…

(1992)

# HELLO

Yeah, it's me here again…
Lost in thought, holding pen.
So jotting, and rotting, I go…
For there's not much else I really know!
Did you see me this day?
How I turned and looked away?
Pretending - a word used often by me.
Just a little understanding,
Could set me free.
One thing I do know is this:
Save your soul, for it is the only thing
That you have any control over.

(1992)

# IMPORTANT REVIEW

How does Shame fade away?
Such Confusion, letting go.
I just want to believe in something for Me.
It's been this way for so Long...
Can hardly remember when it began,
And can't remember life before.
I've been Punishing myself forever;
And I'm not sure I want to stop.
Innocently Abused and Violated...
And I can't stop feeling I was wrong.
A Terrible, Filthy Child of Lies and Hate.
Hiding myself, my life.
Taking on Masks and Admired Traits...
Soon became my way.
I learned what response, what laugh was desired.
And I Forget my childhood and the boundary of reality.

My life has been Demolished, and I want to be Good.
I only feel Shame Burning in my soul
Unable to love such a Filthy child...
And sure no one else could.
I hid her, covered tight, trying to please - and hating it.
Now I see myself as a child, Frightened, Muffled.
Hardly there, but the vision is there all the same.

She calls me now, haunts me, turning me Bitter.
Hope seeps through, where it disappeared last,
Dealing now, with the children of my past.
Frozen in memory each time…
Together they fight me with their shame.
Masks drop, but just slightly, not knowing me…
Learning to face life as Me - Who am I?
And to shed myself of the Torturing Pain.

(1992)

## JUST WONDERING...

Have you ever felt like not going on?
Like never walking out the door?
Have you ever felt the stab of Failure, of Pain?
Would you carry on, just the same?
Have you ever wondered where your courage went?
Do you find you think too much?
That you're about to break with just one more touch?
Have you ever had a day when everything is negative?
Feel tired and lost, and hurt?
Yet out the door you go, trudging through an ocean storm,
Facing the unknown with an open wound,
Bracing for the stinging salt,
As the mist of the world envelops you.

(1992)

# HOVERING

I see the lies you feed.
And the faces you wear.
Come, follow, bleed;
Growing like a weed.
Attraction, confusion, and love…
Time staggers on,
Sowing its truth daggers.
Tomorrow is back to normal,
Not a thing out of place.
Just an illusion, a face.
Never really know the truth…
And carry an awful lot of mace.
Silently covering,
Endlessly hovering.

(1992)

# MY LITTLE GIRL

I can hear her around the corner,
Through the walls in the corridor.
There she lay, crumpled and hurt.
Poor little girl, always alone - yeah.
The man came again and hurt her bad.
Hurt her body and he hurt her heart.
Made her scream and he made her bleed.
But don't you worry, baby, I'm all you need.

'Cause you're my little girl
Ain't no way no man's gonna hurt you that way again
Ain't no way no man's gonna hurt you tonight.
I am here now and I'm gonna make it right.

He's called her daddy, her step-daddy, too.
The man who drove the bus was also the same...
They all controlled her with shame.
Stumblin' from man to man, not even known' a name.
Crying out her fear, cryin' out her pain!
Knowing they are out there lurking', just waitin'.
Afraid that she deserves it, not knowing to say no,
As if she thought it was a thing that she chose.

But you're my little girl
Ain't no way no man's gonna hurt you that way again.
Ain't no way no man's ever gonna hurt you that way again.
My little girl.

(1993)

# OW!!!

A series of disasters
Been bestowed on me
A chain of events
Another catastrophe.
I felt my highest then
Was training to supervise
I worked hard for that job…
My own fears and faults,
I had begun to face.
When a car threw me off my bike…
Ruined my career and my knee.
It will never heal the same.
Limited, poor, and in misery, I suffer.
The lawyers - they fight over what I am due…
Charging up as much as they can.
Insurance Company demands their share too,
To replace the money they finally let go.
Never thinking of the victim…
Only their pockets the publicity and implications.
While I suffered penniless, jobless.
Knowing my career choice has been limited.
I cry for the unjustness of it all.
Pity and rage boil up in one pot…
And I bow my head in the steam and sway;
For being undermined in so many ways.

(1993)

# PATIENCE

Time takes its toll,
Fighting endless cycles
Within the whole
Seeming to slow down
Giving up is tempting
Staying is hard to do.
Feeling ashamed
Of the titles I hold
Feeling tired and old
Yet like a child
Whose heart is wild
And temper is hot
For patience...
Patience is never learned.

(1993)

# TWENTY-THREE

Today is my birthday, 1993,
I am 23 years old.
Still have not let go of the anger I feel
As each childhood assumption is crushed.
People drive me crazy.
I expect too much,
Not willing to let my guard down.
I react to human touch,
Smothering its effect on me.
Out there is a world I had asked to learn
To accept and understand others
So I can blame them and turn on them
With just cause and not doubt.

Tired of feeling criticized for what I do,
Or didn't do when I should have.
Needing acceptance.
Looking for an escape route,
I travel blind.
Placing myself in a padded cell,
I create a world I hate,
Making it easier to remain angry…
And afraid to risk it's comforts.
Feeling meek, small, insignificant, blind.

I am proud of many accomplishments,
Much of which I found difficult
And yet I managed to amaze myself with renewed strength.
I completed a hospitality management program
And was voted valedictorian of the class.
I completed Mathematics 10 and Social Studies 11.
Completed a college course based on self-awareness,
To gain a better perspective towards a career decision.
I created my own garden,
which I have not done on my own before.
I learned a lot about the needs for different plants.
I have maintained a concrete relationship,
Which provides me with the security, support and happiness
That I have needed all these years.
Learning to communicate - though it comes not at all easily.
I have even begun to actually enjoy cooking.
I have proved my resilience, adaptability…

I think some day I may be able to believe in me.

(1993)

# BEING FORGOTTEN

I'm so terribly frightened of what's to come some day,
Afraid that I will die forgotten, in a violent and painful way.
Doing my chores and daily routine, with conscientious flare,
House cleaning, laundry, yard work and more.
Cooking, and baking and washing the car.
The garbage day, recycling and shopping, too.
Trying to complete grade 12 as fast as I can,
Too old to be in high school; too young to commit to a man.
Almost 24, and no babies just yet.
Flying around, in circles - never content.
And I sit here feeling young, tired and poor.
Feeling left behind, frantically groping...
Being young, yet old, at 24.

(1994)

# BITTER YEARS

A college professor
A master of words
A strong young man, once,
Of passion and pain,
Turned old and faded away.

I read his work today,
Sweet poetry from his past.
Confusing how he used his words,
A jumble of old phrases,
Yet the meaning came through anyway.

It saddened me to feel his losses.
His life was full of high costs,
So seemingly short - and bitter
His relentless life was tossed,
A tarnished bit of beaten glitter.

His book told of his passions, and fears
And revealed his exhausted, unshed tears.
The people he knew throughout the years,
Did not really know him at all,
Making me question my meager existence.

Our foolish fragile conditions of life,
A life too short and too easily forgotten;
And of too few delights.
So alone, I cry to this deep night,
For all those bitter years he lived.

(1994)

# HOW CAN THEY BE SO CRUEL?

Yeah, I heard from a friend
Mother Earth's life will end...
In explosions of death, sorrow and pain.
And they tell me the cause is men.
How can they be so cruel?

Yeah they hurt her, and purge her,
They burn her, and poison her rain...
They chop her down, right down to the ground,
Tell me now, why aren't they ashamed?
How can they be so cruel?

Don't all children treat their mothers
With anger and blame
They'll hurt her, abuse her,
'Til she cries out her pain.
Her restless children - untamed.

Now these children fight one-another each and every day,
They are consumed with their own personal gain.
So they rob her and rape her, 'til she bows down.
And there's nothing but unfertile ground.
Her violent children - untamed.

Now this mother, like all mothers,
Forgives all that she can.
And she still holds out her nurturing hand.
Though she dies, we just build more tools…
How can we be so cruel?

Yeah, we rape her, we purge her, and poison her rains.
Cut her forests, burn her soil and feed on her grains.
We are stealing her soul, it's beyond her control…
We've got to stop it somehow…stop it right now!
How could we be so cruel?

(1994)

# JUST GET OVER IT???!!

I hear you men say just get over it.
I heard you say it clear.
Why do you let it rule your life?
Why do you live in fear?
Well, you don't know what it is like,
To feel the touch of a burning knife.
And no matter what you try,
They take you over, and over, and over...
And you don't know what it is like,
To feel vulnerable all the time.
To fear the potential crime,
In every male eye you meet.
So go ahead, sit there and judge.
And tell us how weak we are.
And you feel free to criticize,
Because it makes you feel larger inside.
But until you know what it's like,
You have no right to criticize,
It is not an excuse to be used...
It's just purely and simply abuse.
The victim's life is consistently ruled,
By our confusion of intimacy.
Feeling inadequate and shunned,
Never trustful of our surroundings.
And it is men like you, who criticize
Who try to chop us smaller in size,
That really deserve to know the truth
That bitter blade can bring.

(1995)

# HAPPENSTANCE

Minding my own business, coming home from work,
When, *WHAM!* there you were; *DAMN!* there you were.
How much you've changed - you look unwell.
I remember how you put me through hell.
How much I wanted to yell an insult,
To make you feel some shame!
But once I looked a little closer,
I realized Karma had struck again.
Yeah, you can't even meet my eye,
As you hide behind your hat.
Maybe it's because you've realized,
You really aren't all That.
Telling lies to make your wrongs seem right.
You always belittled me,
To display your courage and might.
Enough of a fool to feel cool.
Though you slept around,
I am here, standing sound,
As you shiver under your hat.
Yeah, you can't even meet my eye!
Behind your hat you try to hide!
And you try to slink away unnoticed,
As if your presence could be denied.
And you stand there with a child by your side

One who looks much like I did then.
But you wouldn't even hold her hand...
As she stares, trying to comprehend.
I see recognition in her eyes and her stance,
The way she asks without words, in her stare...
While you hide behind your hat, in denial...
And I relish this moment of happenstance.

(1995) - Ode to Darcy

# LACKING

I feel once in a while,
Like I've missed something vital;
Something wonderfully exciting.
A clown - funny face; oh, useless one…
Hating this boredom I receive,
Knowing it's just what I prayed for.
Taking advantage of what advantages
I have ever been given…
Restless soul in my heart - bleeding.
Demanding and jealously pleading.

(1995)

# SHE WILL UNDERSTAND

He never really believed it could end this way
He loved her very much, and probably hated her a bit too.
But he never thought she'd suffer so - to end this way…
He couldn't watch her tormenting end…
She will understand.
He wants to remember her stubbornness, her power…
He wants to remember her lively demands.
She is gone now - a relief, yet he grieves.
And he feels sorrow for what may be left unsaid,
The grudges that forever remain - and he suffers.
He lost his only son to drugs,
And his good friend died of old age.
His brother gets cancer and endures treatments.
And now, he silently suffers in his chosen solitude.
And he hungers for life and love but he is afraid.
He finds comfort in his solitude
She will understand.

(1995) Ode to Alfred
*This wonderful man was going through so much this year - I wrote this in my sad attempt to encompass what I thought must be going on in his head.

# THEIR BLAME

There are those of us, who have no idea where they are going,
And still others - well, I don't even want to know.
Those who are doing the same old thing,
Over and over and over again.
Those who cry the same bitter tears,
For all they could have, should have had.
And those who cannot face their fears,
Blaming everyone they meet;
A viscous angle they use to cover their shame.
A blinding front of wounding criticism;
All because they cannot face themselves.

(1995)

# TWENTY-FIVE

My adult life has just begun.
I am now healthier, ready to run.
But to where I ask, here in my room?
Where I dream forbidden thoughts;
And feel guilt for them afterwards.
Who would know the shames I feel?
I feel unsure of what I should be.
And I wonder why the woman's curse,
Turns emotions upside down.
Why, I also wonder, I frown on,
What my girlfriend is or has on.
And why I see less in so many others.
I hate the fact that I even doubt,
In the man that I have chosen to love.
Whether he is as true, and good, as I believe.
And I for him - who knows?
I dwell on my weaknesses…
Behind closed doors, I yell it!
And I fear for my future…
Whether success is really in store,
If I will ever own a house with land;
And if I do, will it be because of a man?
Will I work forever? Or be a mom? Or do nothing?
Will I combine them all and grow old too fast?
And on top of it all, I must wake up tomorrow.
Probably not even remembering tonight's sorrow.
And I will carry on with the mundane day,
As its events slam into me.

(1995)

# BEGUILING YOUTH

Self-criticism denies me experiences while shame holds me in my past.
Doubt in social circles leads me to my own grounds where thoughts are cast.
Shadowed by a hint of sorrow my glee over my acquirements dwindles.
A sense of an invasive realism blossoms, firmly melting fiction away.
And as I stand in a puddle of wholesome ideals once preached,
I insanely stamp in it, sending it splattering to the heated ground,
So that it sizzles away with my anger.
And rising, the steam reaches for the stars…
And as it rises I dare it to return in showers of answers and brilliant justice…
Which will cool my fury over the beguiling innocence of youth.

(1996)

# Locomotion

Locomotion keeps me moving through the confusing compulsive waves of life.
And lost in this rush, I consume and exhaust myself for the unknown.
Feeling awfully tired I pause and look in at my routines in disgust.
And a desperate yearning to escape beyond the maze and into self-sufficiency arises.

(1996)

# OUR SUN SHINES

How can we fight it, when so many deny it?
When in our blind little world,
Our sun shines.
Every researcher, every study, every survey;
Has both a motive and a contradiction;
But our sun shines.
It is money that dictates who should be denied,
And it is money which dictates who's to be tried;
But our sun shines.
There's so many pharmacies; supplying too many drugs,
For illnesses we helped create.
But our sun shines.
We submit to governments in our bewildered state.
Blissfully blinded we consume our toxic waste.
But our sun shines.
Our glorious blue skies fuel our stupefied haste,
To get whatever we can from this bright, sunny place.
How brightly it shines.

(1996)

# DEATH

When age prompts you to look back on your life,
Will you see a pleasure earned for every strife?
...or will you care?
Will you remember any childhood days?
Will you see in them some very happy days?
...or will you care?
Will you find pride in your monetary things?
Will they exchange for some very pretty wings?
...or will you care?
Will emotional ties follow on your ride?
Will they hold you down, or let you fly?
...or will you care?
When you look to the loves of your life,
Will there be regret reflected in your eyes?
...or will you care?
Are you ready to be taken from your life -
Would you accept it, or would you fight?
...or would you care?

(1997)

# PURPOSE?

Is there a purpose for us all?
Do we learn each time we stumble and fall?
And as we bleed, do we feel appreciation?
Bleeding, we suffer our own creation…
Shallow little hearts beat out sophisticated lives;
Lungs wheezing air in our polluted hives.
Bitter bile churns and chars our core,
As we worry and bite, how to take more.
Purpose in chaos - or a religious dream?
Disorganized intentions push us upstream.
And perilous waters carry our tiny hives,
Through the whirlpools of our pressured lives.

(1997)
*Published '02 National Library of Poetry, Poetry Institute of Canada: Hardcover Anthology: *Shadows of the Dawn*

# THE WORKING POOR

We will dig ourselves some grit,
And with cardboard spoons,
And with our stiffened hands,
We will work to find a spec of gold.
Never forgetting what's bought and sold.
Ever neglecting those we've worked to hold.
Forcing us on, the longing taking us there.
It's always lurking and beyond our control.
The pan grows rusty and holes appear,
Where the stones wore their way clear,
A pan, once new - once brought dreams,
Today - brings little more than despair.
Wondering where the paths we seek,
Could have hidden from our blistered feet.
The labyrinth shines well beyond our doors…
We are called the lost and the working poor.

(1997)

# FROZEN IN TIME

Denise, you were a friend of mine…
Right from the start, we were one in our hearts,
Way back then.
I remember, you and I, in the deep, deep snow,
Desperately searching the sky for UFOs.
Anything to make our lives exciting.
Always feeling alone, 'til our friendship came along.
Then one day I was called back home,
Returning to a broken, but safe home;
Was not sure if I liked it better this way.
Felt terribly alone - a stranger there.
And I think of you, every couple of years - I do;
Of our friendship - you and I - frozen in time.

(1999)

# Change of Weather

There's a change of weather coming...
I can feel it in my bones.
This muffled white serenity,
Is settling my soul.
There's a change of weather coming...
And it's aiming at my bones.
The ache of pressure separating
Is muffled by a coat of snow.
There's a change of weather coming...
A cold, cold rush of anticipation,
And the icy winds' sensation,
Burns into the marrow of my bones.

(2000)

# 30 AND GRATEFUL

Once, I felt absorbed in self-pity
For a long, involved stage in my life
A feeling some may say was justified.
I had no father, knew hunger and lived poor.
Abusive men sought this easy target,
Handily near - shy and full of fear.
Each time I told, I felt inferior…
Like I had done the wrong.
One spent time in jail - the other is free,
Because I couldn't face the shame in court.
My family, a walking wounded group
Separated - yearning for connection.
I raised myself, alone.
A child paying rent - schooling myself,
Getting into trouble…
Now, at 30, I can see past the pain to what was good.
I have experienced parts of California, Nevada, BC and the NWT.
I have seen Knott's Berry Farm, Disneyland and the Armstrong Fair!
Felt the thrill of suspended height, the rush of wind in my hair.
I had a wonderful foster parent who cared,
Put me in school and in a girls' abuse group,
Where, for a while, I learned to be a kid.
It could have been so much worse -
I could have become a hooker, a criminal, an addict or dead.
I had wonderful friends, who protected me instead.
Because of them, I knew things could be better.
So I took courses, had counseling and read books.
Anything to come to terms with my hate, anger, hurt and fears.

Enabling me to commit to a wonderful man,
Who completes me.
Despite the injuries incurred from 3 accidents,
And the subsequent loss of 2 careers;
I remain happy and comfortable in my life.
Grateful am I to have learned of my self.
It has been hard - but how many have had this chance?
I am 30 and I am Grateful.

(April, 2001)

# CONTRADICTION

Governments are fundamentally unsustainable for our nation.
Sweetened words rot while panels point fingers in every direction.
Implicitly implying our hunger, our homes are worth the risk.
Ensuring the dependants and unproductive ones suffer most,
Our society initially caused this appendage host.
Small islands, we like to call parks, become our only wild lands.
Murdering creative spirits, society crushes and smears the people.
Children, not even safe from their own family members,
Are taught to conform to patterns acceptable to the masses.
Struggling to directionalize their aim; it's there, but there it's not.
Living lives in contradiction - confinement where the spirit soars.
Keeping open receptors; we armor our selves with our only swords.
Those bright neon lights meant to aid our choice in direction,
Only blend in the masses of society's blinking illuminations.
Our culture collision ridicules all beliefs while entwining them all.
And peacefully inflicting our belief of justice and virtues on one another,
Our own violence and war feeds our senseless economy and dependence.
And finding a tiny flower in a crack between cement and men,
We become inspired to save it.

(2001)

# WILLOW ROAD GOODBYES

This heart ached as I watched them go
Visiting was like a fresh forest rain.
His poem of goodbye a reminder
Of the eminent end
Excitement and fear share whispers
That vibrate my physical fibers
Feeling taut, yet happy - yet sad.
Afraid I won't like this dream
We've had for so long.
Isolation, a tool for the writer
A dream that eases fear…
But could it worsen?
I wonder.
A long winter to settle in a new home
To press further into creation; into my soul
A time to mold and condition the body
To fill the mind; entertain the spirit.
To plan for the new season to come.
What to order and what to plant where.
Where to build the greenhouse,
The cold-frame; prepare for warm air.
For now to remain calm,
To appreciate the peace,
And flow with our move…
This is the battle I face.

(October 31, 2001)
*Written just after a visit from Dave's parents at a home we had just moved to and at a time when we were working with our publishers on our book, *Trash Talk*.

# ODE TO BC

Floating, swirling, swooping in clean skies,
Above turquoise and emerald encrusted mountains,
They soar among the currents - diving for their meals.
Playing under clouds and wisps of spring rains
BC's winged angels guard a natural treasure.
The green-gold of Canada's jewel
Lures the world to pan our wonders.
Yet this diversity, our sweet and bitter core,
Teaches us to embrace and nourish the mountain lakes;
Where bears roam and cougars roar…
And the shy lynx dance along to music
Made by trickling streams and rushing rivers,
That lead to the ocean lapping at our shore.
With hope and love in mankind's hearts,
We relish in knowing this wilderness exists…
Surviving us.

(2002)
*This is the only poem I have ever written that did not flow from my pen. After hearing about a contest on CBC Radio for poems about the province of BC, I decided to try to write one. This was a completely new approach for me to do, and by the time I had completed it to my satisfaction - the contest had been over with for some time!

# OUR HANDS

I'm standing here
Wondering what is out there for us
And I am looking back
At the successes we have had,
And the things that we have gained.
Through all the pain,
We have withstood it all…
Hand in hand.

(2002)

* A dedication to the strength and flexibility of the relationship I share with my husband – we have been together for 15 years, as of the printing of this book.

# TRUE KNOWLEDGE

Each of us are motivated either by intuition or self-servance.
Dented and buffered by our distinct memories,
Which are shaped by our context of experience,
We struggle to find understanding in structured society.
Who says structure has anything to do with reason?
Society is really based on what we do not know.
Yet we generously share knowledge internationally.
So understanding little we grope for leaders, heroes…
When what we need are active citizens.
Unstifled imagination - it is the tool of certainty.
One era's ethics only corrupt future generations.
Nonconformity is an insult, a sign of disloyalty to society…
But does true knowledge belong only to scholars?
True understanding comes not from a degree.
Not from stretching our small mouths to fit,
A vocabulary we are meant to recite.
We are the heroes that we seek. You and I.
What are you doing in your life? That is where it lies.
Does this mean money? I think not.
Does it mean good deeds? Maybe.
I believe it lies in understanding and accepting - before judging or acting.
It lies in the heart - in the mind…
Settled in self and matter around us.
A society of followers, of conformists, of memorizers and repeaters.
Why repeat what has been done before?
Be a hero.
Act today.
Create.

(2002)

# MOTHER-IN-LAW

Plump, rounded and plain
Her beautiful eyes shone.
Feigning, she hid a sharp mind.
...Quietly watchful...
Kind and innocent in so many ways,
Yet the woman bore worldly hurts in her time.
Ever fretting over her spawn and forgetting about herself.
Frail and vexed with age – her resilience reigned.
I saw her children gather...
...family showing family support.

My heart wrenches; stomach clenches,
...at our impending loss.
Visualizing funerals and gatherings...
...saying useless things.
Claustrophobic walls; medical smells...
Feebly letting her go and begin to somehow rise...
Rise with whatever strength we learned,
Whatever resilience she passed on to us all...
And carry on, knowing we were blessed
To have had moments with her in our lifetime.

(June 26, 2003) – Ode to Marlene